P9-CMX-232

		DATE DUE		

THE CHICAGO PUBLIC LIBRARY

WEST CHICAGO BRANCH
4844 W. CHICAGO AVE.
CHICAGO, IL 60651

Animal Rescuers

A CHAPTER BOOK

BY ROSANNA HANSEN

children's press®

A Division of Scholastic Inc.
New York Toronto London Auckland Sydney
Mexico City New Delhi Hong Kong
Danbury, Connecticut

For Emmalyn and Rebecca,
cousins extraordinaire

ACKNOWLEDGMENTS

The author would like to thank the human and animal heroes whose brave deeds and kindness are the inspiration for this book. Many thanks and best wishes go to Philip and Ginny Gonzalez; Scarlett and her friends at the North Shore Animal League; LuLu and Jo Ann Altsman; Salty and Omar Rivera; and Donna Enright. Thanks also to Mighty Mony, who appears on the cover of this book, as well as Mony's handler, Detective Jonni Joyce of the Raleigh-Durham International Airport Police.

Library of Congress Cataloging-in-Publication Data

Hansen, Rosanna.
  Animal rescuers : a chapter book / by Rosanna Hansen.
    p. cm. – (True tales)
Summary: Describes four animal heroes: Ginny, a dog who helps cats;
Scarlett, a cat who rescued her kittens from fire; Lulu, a pig who found
help for her ill owner; and Dorado, a guide dog who led his owner out of
the collapsing World Trade Center on September 11, 2001.
Includes bibliographical references and index.
  ISBN 0-516-22915-X (lib. bdg.)   0-516-24602-X (pbk.)
  1. Pets–Anecdotes–Juvenile literature. 2. Domestic animals–Anecdotes–Juvenile litera-
ture. 3. Animal heroes–Anecdotes–Juvenile literature. [1. Animal heroes–Anecdotes. 2.
Pets–Anecdotes. 3. Domestic animals–Anecdotes.] I. Title. II. Series.

  SF416.2.H35 2003
  636.088'7–dc21

                              2003003720

© 2003 Nancy Hall, Inc.
Published in 2003 by Children's Press
A Division of Scholastic Inc.
All rights reserved. Published simultaneously in Canada.
Printed in the United States of America.

CHILDREN'S PRESS and associated logos are trademarks and or registered trademarks
of Scholastic Library Publishing. SCHOLASTIC and associated logos are trademarks and
or registered trademarks of Scholastic Inc.

1 2 3 4 5 6 7 8 9 10 R 12 11 10 09 08 07 06 05 04 03

CONTENTS

INTRODUCTION

Not all **heroes** are human. Sometimes heroes bark, meow, or even grunt. They may be covered with fur, have curly tails, or live in an alley.

In this book, you will find true stories about four animal heroes. Each of these heroes has performed an amazing **rescue.** Sometimes they even put themselves in danger to help others. Ginny is a dog who rescues stray cats. Scarlett is a brave cat who saved her five kittens from a fire. When her owner had a **heart attack,** LuLu the pig went for help. Salty, a guide dog, led his owner down seventy-one flights of stairs when the **World Trade Center** was attacked.

They may be different shapes and sizes, but these animals all have two things in common. They have all saved lives, and they are all true heroes.

CHAPTER ONE

THE DOG WHO LOVES CATS

Most dogs don't like cats, but Ginny is not an ordinary dog. Ginny loves cats. She loves to help cats who are hurt or **handicapped** (HAN-dee-kapd).

Ginny and her owner, Philip Gonzalez, rescue and care for cats that need help. Every day, they go out to feed the **stray** cats in their town. Along the way, Ginny often finds cats who are hurt or **disabled** (diss-AY-buhld).

Unlike most dogs, Ginny loves cats.

Ginny seems to have a special sense that lets her find these cats. One night, Ginny and Philip were walking by a building under **construction.** Ginny started begging. She wanted to go into the building. Philip finally let her go.

Ginny raced through the building. Soon she returned, holding a tiny kitten in her mouth. She had found the kitten in the air conditioning pipes. The kitten was hurt and couldn't walk. Philip and Ginny took the kitten to the **vet.**

The vet said the kitten would never be able to walk. Philip adopted the kitten and named her Topsy. As Topsy got bigger, she learned a special way to get around. Since she can't walk, she rolls along the floor. She can even roll up and over the edge of her litter box.

Another time, Philip and Ginny were out feeding stray cats. Suddenly, Ginny ran over to a nearby factory building. She stopped by a box full of broken glass. Ginny began digging through the glass. Her paws started to bleed, but Ginny kept digging.

Finally, she stuck her face into the glass. She pulled out a ball of bloody fur and licked it gently. The little fur ball gave a soft **mew.** It was alive!

Every day, Philip Gonzales and Ginny feed stray cats in their town.

**Philip and Ginny live in an apartment
with all the cats they have adopted.**

Philip took Ginny and the kitten home to clean their cuts and scratches. After a few days, Philip decided to adopt the kitten. Philip named him the Chairman, because he acted so **independent** (in-di-PEN-duhnt).

Whenever Ginny finds a disabled cat, Philip finds it a home or adopts it himself. The first cat he adopted was Madame. She is deaf in both ears. Then Ginny found Revlon. She has only one eye. Next there was Betty Boop, who was born without hind feet. Later, Topsy and the Chairman joined the group.

Ginny's friend Rufus

Philip and Ginny

Today, Philip and Ginny share their home with Topsy, the Chairman, Madame, Revlon, Betty Boop, and other adopted cats. Ginny loves all the cats. She spends hours **grooming** and playing with them.

Philip first met Ginny when he went to an **animal shelter** to look for a dog. Ginny had been starved and **abandoned** (uh-BAN-duhnd) as a young dog. She had been taken to the shelter to get her strength back.

Philip was drawn to Ginny right away. He liked her pretty face and bright eyes. However, he wasn't sure he wanted to adopt Ginny. He was looking for a bigger dog. That didn't matter, because Ginny decided to adopt him! She looked at Philip, wagged her tail, and licked his fingers. Philip soon decided that Ginny was just the right dog for him.

Philip and Ginny have been together for many years. Every day, they go out and feed more than two hundred stray cats in their town of Long Beach, New York. Philip has set up several feeding places around the town. His friend Sheilah Harris helps with the feedings. She also adopts some of the cats.

A few years ago, Philip started The Ginny Fund. This fund gives money to pay the vets who care for the cats. It also helps Philip find good homes for as many cats as possible.

Philip says that Ginny has helped him find a sense of purpose. He also says he is lucky to have an amazing dog like Ginny, a dog who rescues cats.

CHAPTER TWO

SCARLETT, THE BRAVE CAT

Have you ever watched a building burn down on television? If you have, you know fires are scary. The flames and smoke from a fire are terrifying for both humans and animals.

In March 1996, a stray cat in New York City somehow overcame her fear of fire. She ran into a burning building five times to save her kittens. Her fur and paws got burned on the hot coals.

Firefighters at work

**The building in New York City where
Scarlett rescued her kittens**

David Giannelli found Scarlett and her kittens.

Her eyes began to **blister** from the heat, but the brave mother rescued her whole family. Then she **collapsed.**

Meanwhile, firefighters from Hook and Ladder Company 175 worked to put out the blaze. At last, the fire was under control. The firefighters began to pack up. Suddenly, firefighter David Giannelli heard some soft mews. He found five tiny kittens near the building. Their fur was smoky and **scorched.**

Where was the mother cat? David finally found her across the street. She lay gasping for breath. She was badly burned over much of her body. David found a box and gently placed the mother and babies inside.

David could see that the cats needed a vet. He rushed them to a nearby shelter called the North Shore Animal League.

The animal shelter where Scarlett and her kittens were rushed

Scarlett and her kittens

David decided to name the brave mother cat Scarlett because she had red patches in her spotted fur.

At the shelter, several vets examined Scarlett and the kittens. They were worried that Scarlett might die from her burns. Even if she lived, Scarlett might be blinded by the blisters on her eyes.

The kittens were in better shape. The vets thought they had a good chance of living. For many days, the shelter **staff** cared for Scarlett and the kittens.

Dr. Larry Cohen examines Scarlett.

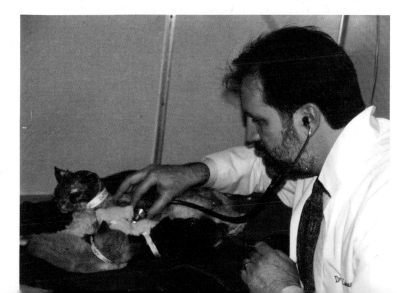

By the third day, the blisters on Scarlett's eyes had started to **heal**. Scarlett could open her eyes a little. She could see! The vets were happy that she was better. The kittens were getting better, too. They slept, ate, and drank milk from tiny bottles.

News reporters around the world wrote about Scarlett's brave rescue. Over six thousand people called the animal shelter. They called to ask if they could adopt Scarlett and her kittens. Scarlett was famous.

After their first week at North Shore, three of the kittens suddenly became sick. Two of the kittens got well, but one kitten died. Everyone at North Shore was very sad.

Scarlett and her kittens stayed at North Shore for three more months. Scarlett's burns healed, and most of her fur grew back. The kittens got big and playful. It was time for Scarlett and her family to get homes of their own.

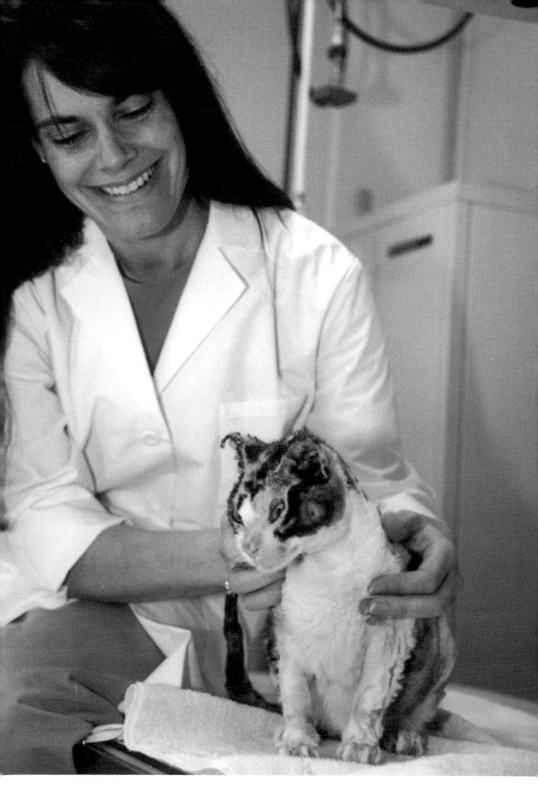

Lexi Funderberg and the staff at North Shore
Animal League nursed Scarlett back to health.

The staff at North Shore read hundreds of letters from people who wanted the cats. Finally the staff chose several lucky families. Scarlett and her babies went to different homes. The staff thought that Scarlett needed some peace and quiet.

Today, Scarlett and her children are doing well. They are healthy, happy, and enjoying life with their human families.

Karen Weller was chosen from many people who wanted to adopt Scarlett.

**Tanuki (at left) and Samsara (at right),
two of Scarlett's kittens**

**Oreo (at left) and Cinders (at right),
Scarlett's two other kittens**

In 1996, Scarlett was named Feline Heroine of the Year by the International Cat Association.

CHAPTER THREE

LULU TO THE RESCUE

LuLu is a **pot-bellied pig.** These pigs have become popular pets. They are usually smaller than farm pigs and they are very smart. Their owners say these pigs make loyal, loving friends.

LuLu is a special pot-bellied pig that proved that this is certainly true. One summer, LuLu and her owner, Jo Ann Altsman, were on vacation. They were staying at their holiday home in Presque Isle in Pennsylvania. Suddenly, Jo Ann had a **heart attack.**

Pot-bellied pigs are loyal, loving pets.

LuLu with Jo Ann Altsman

Jo Ann's chest began to hurt, and she fell to the floor in terrible pain. "Somebody, please help me!" she cried. LuLu came running to her side.

At first, LuLu laid her head on Jo Ann's chest and cried. Then LuLu squeezed through the dog's door and into the yard. LuLu had never left the yard before, but this day would be different. Somehow LuLu opened the gate. Then she ran out into the street.

LuLu stood waiting in the street until she saw a car. Then she lay down right in front of the car. The driver stopped, but was afraid to get out of his car. He had never seen a pig hogging the road before!

A second driver stopped his car and got out. LuLu was causing her own traffic jam, and she seemed to know what to do next. She quickly led the man up to the house.

The man knocked on the door, and Jo Ann heard him. "Please call 911," she cried.

An ambulance arrived a few minutes later. Even then, LuLu didn't think her job was done. She tried to get into the ambulance with Jo Ann. The **medics** had to tell the brave pig to stay home. LuLu had helped enough for one day.

At the hospital, Jo Ann got the medicine and care she needed. Her doctors told her LuLu had probably saved her life. If even fifteen more minutes had gone by, Jo Ann might have died. Soon Jo Ann was able to go home and be with LuLu again.

How did Jo Ann thank LuLu for her help? She gave LuLu a jelly doughnut, one of Lulu's favorite foods. LuLu was also awarded the **ASPCA** Trooper Award for Bravery.

LuLu's favorite treat

CHAPTER FOUR

SALTY AND THE FALLING BUILDING

Dogs have often been known for their **courage** and loyalty. Throughout history, many dogs have put themselves in danger to save a human friend. This is a true story about a brave dog named Salty and his owner, Omar Rivera.

Omar Rivera with Salty

Omar works as a **computer technician** (tek-NISH-uhn) in New York City. Omar is blind. So, he takes his guide dog, Salty, to work. Salty is trained to help Omar anywhere they go.

Omar worked in the north tower of the World Trade Center. His office was on the 71st floor. On September 11, 2001, he was sitting at his desk. An airplane hit the tower 25 floors above him.

When the plane hit, Omar jumped up. He could hear glass and metal breaking. He could feel smoke and heat filling his lungs. Omar knew it would be hard for him to escape. He didn't think he could get out of the building.

An airplane hit the north tower of the World Trade Center.

Omar decided to let Salty go free. He wanted the dog to have a chance to escape. Omar unclipped the dog's lead and told him to run. Meanwhile, people were rushing past them toward the stairs. Glass was breaking and walls were cracking. People were screaming and running.

In the confusion, Salty was swept away by a crowd of people. Omar was alone. A few minutes later, Omar had a surprise. He felt Salty nudge his leg. The dog had come back to help his master.

With Salty at his side, Omar began the long trip down the stairs. On the way, Omar met Donna Enright, a woman who worked with him. Donna offered to help Omar. He put one hand on Donna's arm. He put the other hand on Salty's harness. Then the three of them walked down the stairs together.

It took over an hour for Omar, Donna, and Salty to walk down seventy flights of stairs. At first, the people around them were pushing and shoving them. Then, as Omar and his helpers kept going, people started to calm down.

Finally, Omar, Donna, and Salty reached the ground. They hurried away to safety. Before long, the building collapsed.

Omar had been amazed when Salty came back for him. Omar said, "I knew for certain he loved me just as much as I loved him. He was prepared to die in the hope he might save my life." As Omar puts it, Donna Enright and Salty were his angels that terrible day.

Omar and Salty reached safety before the building collapsed.

September 11, 2001, was a terrible day in New York City. Many firefighters, police officers, and other people who were nearby, rushed to help the people who were trapped in the World Trade Center. There were many dogs who worked hard to help, too.

Three of these dogs were given an important award for their work that day. They were awarded the Dickin Medal by the British government. This medal is the highest honor Great Britain gives to an animal who is brave when faced with danger.

Salty was one of two guide dogs presented with the medal at this ceremony. The other was Roselle, who was able to get her master down seventy-eight floors to safety.

Apollo was the third dog. He was one of the bravest police dogs that helped the people in the World Trade Center on September 11, 2001.

GLOSSARY

abandoned (uh-BAN-duhnd) left behind

animal shelter a place where unwanted animals are cared for

ASPCA The American Society for the Prevention of Cruelty to Animals

blister a bubble on the skin caused by a burn

collapsed broke down or caved in

computer technician (tek-NISH-uhn) someone who fixes computers

construction the act of building something

courage the ability to face danger bravely

disabled (diss-AY-buhld) not being able to do what you want to do because you are ill or injured in some way

grooming washing or brushing an animal

guide dog a dog trained to help blind people get around

handicapped (HAN-dee-kapd) having a disability of the body

heal to make or become well

heart attack what happens when not enough blood reaches the heart

heroes people or animals admired for having been brave

independent (in-di-PEN-duhnt) free from the control of other people

medics people who are trained to help others in emergencies

pot-bellied pig a kind of pig that is very smart and is popular as a pet

rescue to save someone who is in trouble

scorched something that is burned on top

staff a group of people who work together

stray an animal that is lost or without a home

vet (short for veterinarian) a doctor who treats animals

World Trade Center seven buildings in New York City with two very tall towers that were attacked and collapsed in 2001

FIND OUT MORE

The Dog Who Loves Cats
www.theginnyfund.org
This site tells about Ginny, Philip Gonzalez, and the fund in Ginny's honor.

Scarlett, the Brave Cat
www.pets-in-the-news.com
Learn more about Scarlett and her kittens, as well as other heroic animals.

LuLu to the Rescue
www.pigs4ever.com
Read articles about LuLu and other interesting pigs.

Other Websites to Visit
www.myhero.com
This site has articles on many animal heroes and human heroes.

More Books to Read
Dog to the Rescue: Seventeen True Tales of Dog Heroism by Jeanette Sanderson, Scholastic, 1993

Ten True Animal Rescues by Jeanne Betancourt, Econo-Clad Books, 1998

Animals to the Rescue!: True Stories of Animal Heroes by Christopher Farran, HarperCollins Children's Books, 2000

INDEX

PHOTO CREDITS

Cover copyright © Jen Bidner/binder@mail.com

3, 7, 15 Mary Boolm

4 (top left), **6, 9, 12, 19** Laura Miller

1, 4 (top right), **17, 18, , 20, 21, 23, 24, 25, 26, 27** Courtesy of Mary Bloom/North Shore Animal League

4 (bottom left), **33** Larry Lettera/Feature Photo Service

4 (bottom right), **34, 38** Joe McNally

16 CORBIS

28 G.K. & Vikki Hart/PhotoDisc/PictureQuest

29 Vicky Kasala/PhotoDisc/PictureQuest

30 UPI Photo Service

32 Stockbyte/PictureQuest

35 PDSA Britain's leading vetinary charity

36 George Weld/www.likeanorb.com

41 Reuters Pictures Archive

43 Associated Press

MEET THE AUTHOR

Rosanna Hansen has worked in children's publishing as a manager, editor, and author. Most recently, she was publisher and editor in chief of Weekly Reader, supervising seventeen classroom magazines as well as book publishing. Previously, she was group publisher of Reader's Digest Children's Books.

Hansen has written a number of children's books, including several on animals. She is also a volunteer with the Good Dog Foundation, which trains therapy dogs.

She and her husband, Corwith, live in Tuckahoe, New York.

THE _____ LIBRARY